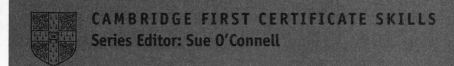
CAMBRIDGE FIRST CERTIFICATE
Writing

NEW EDITION

drew

Lawday

Teacher's Book

CAMBRIDGE
UNIVERSITY PRESS

PUBLISHED BY THE PRESS SYNDICATE OF THE UNIVERSITY OF CAMBRIDGE
The Pitt Building, Trumpington Street, Cambridge, United Kingdom

CAMBRIDGE UNIVERSITY PRESS
The Edinburgh Building, Cambridge CB2 2RU, UK
40 West 20th Street, New York, NY 10011–4211, USA
10 Stamford Road, Oakleigh, VIC 3166, Australia
Ruiz de Alarcón 13, 28014 Madrid, Spain
Dock House, The Waterfront, Cape Town 8001, South Africa

http://www.cambridge.org

First published 1993
Second edition 1999
Third printing 2001

Printed in the United Kingdom at the University Press, Cambridge

ISBN 0 521 62484 3 Teacher's Book
ISBN 0 521 62483 5 Student's Book

Contents

Acknowledgements

We would like to thank Charlotte Adams, Niki Browne and Judith Greet for their help in preparing the revised version of the book.

The general impression mark scheme on page 4 is reproduced by kind permission of the University of Cambridge Local Examinations Syndicate.

From the first edition:

We would like to thank the Series Editor, Sue O'Connell, for her invaluable help and guidance, our editor Jeanne McCarten for nursing authors and manuscript through all the various stages, Geraldine Mark, Joanne Currie and the staff at Cambridge University Press for their efforts in the production of the book, and of course the teachers and students who piloted it, for their helpful comments.

Introduction

Who is this book for?

This book provides writing practice for students preparing for the writing paper of the Cambridge FCE exam: Paper 2 (Writing). It may also be used as a general writing skills course. It aims to provide both skills development and exam training; to cover a wide range of topics and functions; to draw students' attention to the 'process' of writing through the stages of planning, writing and improving; to give interesting, motivating tasks.

How is the book organised?

The book is organised into eighteen units. Each unit focuses on a particular type of First Certificate task and concentrates on the language and writing skills students will need for that task.

How is each unit organised?

Each unit starts with a **preview** section introducing the topic dealt with in the unit.

This is followed by a **planning** section which introduces students to one of a variety of planning techniques which they are encouraged to experiment with throughout the course.

Two **skills development** sections follow, providing practice in language and writing skills that students will find useful in performing the writing task.

A further **planning** section gives students the opportunity to put into practice the technique learnt earlier in the unit. This second section can be done in class or, if time is short, for homework along with the exam task.

An **exam-type task**, for use either in class or as homework, provides realistic First Certificate practice.

The unit is completed with an **improving your work** section to be tackled after the writing task is finished. This section encourages students to revise and polish their work. It also gives practical learner training ideas and activities both to help students prepare specifically for the exam and to enable them to develop their writing and general language learning skills.

How should the material be used?

The course may be used in strict unit sequence. Alternatively teachers may wish to develop each exam task type in sequence.

Each unit provides about an hour's pre-task work. There is scope for flexibility, however, and the Teacher's Book suggests ways of extending or reducing the time needed. The exam-type task can be done either in class or for homework. Timed practices of 45 minutes will be necessary towards the exam. The improving section should be done in a follow-up lesson and will take 15–20 minutes depending on the task and how it develops.

What special features are there?

* The book begins with a **Foundation unit** which is designed to increase students' awareness of key aspects of writing.
* Each unit begins with a **Mini-syllabus** to show students exactly which type of exam task and which skills are covered in the unit.
* Each unit contains **Exam Tips** which summarise key points to remember for the exam. Some units also contain **Study Tips** which give useful advice on how to improve your writing generally.
* The detailed **Teacher's Book** provides practical suggestions, ideas for further activities, and guidelines on timing.
* The book finishes with a **Review unit** which brings together as much essential information as possible for a final revision session.

Foundation unit

What are your expectations?

First elicit ideas from students. Then ask them to read through the statements on their own. When they have done this, put them in pairs or groups to discuss their answers. Then have a class feedback session, making sure the following points are also mentioned:
- planning
- revising and polishing
- organisation
- exam requirements

What sorts of writing does the First Certificate exam require?

This exercise is designed to help students develop an awareness of different forms of written English, especially those required by the FCE exam.

> **KEY**   What sorts of writing does the First Certificate exam require?
> 1 narrative
> 2 informal letter
> 3 description (of a place) / informal letter
> 4 report (description of a place)
> 5 description (of a person) / informal letter
> 6 discussion essay
> 7 formal letter
> 8 article

What does the First Certificate exam expect?

Ask students to choose their four most important points and then put students in pairs to compare their answers. When they have finished, have a class discussion of each point. The following information about the marking of the FCE exam may be useful.

The tasks are given an 'impression' mark. This mark is based on the range of structure and vocabulary, the coverage of points required, the organisation and presentation of the task, the control of language and register, and the effect of the task on the target reader. Marks are given for the general impression but there is also a task specific mark scheme focusing on criteria specific to each particular task.

The general impression mark scheme is summarised overleaf.

5	Full realisation of task set. • All content points included. • Wide range of structure and vocabulary within the task set. • Minimal errors, perhaps due to ambition; well-developed control of language. • Ideas effectively organised and paragraphed, with a variety of linking devices. • Register and format consistently appropriate to purpose and audience. Fully achieves the desired effect on the target reader.
4	Good realisation of the task set. • All major content points included; possibly one or two minor omissions. • Good range of structure and vocabulary within the task set. • Generally accurate, errors occur mainly when attempting more complex language. • Ideas clearly organised and paragraphed, with suitable linking devices. • Register and format on the whole appropriate to purpose and audience. Achieves the desired effect on the target reader.
3	Reasonable achievement of the task set. • All major content points included; some minor omissions. • Adequate range of structure and vocabulary, which fulfils the requirements of the task. • A number of errors may be present, but they do not impede communication. • Ideas adequately organised and paragraphed, with simple linking devices. • Reasonable, if not always successful attempt at register and format appropriate to purpose and audience. Achieves, on the whole, the desired effect on the target reader.
2	Task set attempted but not adequately achieved. • Some major content points inadequately covered or omitted, and/or some irrelevant material. • Limited range of structure and vocabulary. • A number of errors, which distract the reader and may obscure communication at times. • Ideas inadequately organised and paragraphed; linking devices rarely used. • Unsuccessful/inconsistent attempts at appropriate register and format. Message not clearly communicated to the target reader.
1	Poor attempt at task set. • Notable content omissions and/or considerable irrelevance, possibly due to misinterpretation of task set. • Narrow range of vocabulary and structure. • Frequent errors which obscure communication; little evidence of language control. • Lack of organisation, paragraph or linking devices. • Little or no awareness of appropriate register and format. Very negative effect on the target reader.
0	Achieves nothing: too little language for assessment (fewer than 50 words) or totally illegible.

Other points to draw students' attention to include:

Spelling: Spelling is important in so far as it contributes to the 'impression' mark. Examiners may adjust the impression mark if they feel that consistently poor spelling impedes communication.

Grammar: Accuracy is one of the main criteria used by examiners when calculating the impression mark. However, examiners do not count every grammatical mistake and deduct marks accordingly. Students should not worry unduly about grammatical accuracy, there are other important factors too.

Answering the question fully/Not leaving out any important points: Candidates can receive top marks if they completely fulfil the task set, covering all the points required. They will receive medium marks if they fulfil the task simply but accurately, covering the main points. They will receive low marks if they have omitted relevant material. If their answer totally fails to answer the task set, they will receive very few marks.

Punctuation: Punctuation is important in so far as it contributes to the 'impression' mark. Examiners may adjust the impression mark if they feel that consistently poor punctuation impedes communication.

Right number of words: Candidates are asked to write 120–180 words and answers that are too short are penalised. For example, an answer that is only half the length asked for is marked out of a maximum of half the available marks for that question. If answers are longer than required, the examiner draws a line at the place where the correct length is reached and marks closely what comes before the line, but also gives some credit for relevant material that comes later.

Register: Candidates should use register that is appropriate to the purpose and the target reader.

Clarity: It is very important that answers are clear. Unclear or confusing answers will create a bad impression.

Legibility: Handwriting is important in so far as it contributes to the 'impression' mark. Examiners may adjust the impression mark if they feel that consistently poor handwriting impedes communication.

Vocabulary: Obviously a good range of vocabulary will impress the examiners, and make the composition more interesting. Students should avoid using words inappropriately in a vain attempt to get more 'long' words into their composition.

Relevance: Candidates who answer the question irrelevantly are penalised. Material that is clearly irrelevant (perhaps learned by heart) or that misinterprets the question is marked out of a smaller maximum number of possible marks.

Layout/Format: Using appropriate layouts and formats, especially for letters and reports, will create a positive impression. A by-product of using appropriate layouts will often be that candidates plan their compositions more carefully.

Effect on the target reader: Candidates should show by their control of the features above that they have identified the target reader and that their writing will have an appropriately positive effect on that reader.

Other information about the FCE exam which students will find useful:

Forms of writing: These will include a letter, a narrative, a description, an exam-type essay, a report or an article. There is also a question based on the optional set book.

Topics: These include jobs and work, school and study, leisure, sport, travel, holidays, your own home or town or country, family and friends, people you know or have met, world issues, accidents and crime, special occasions.

(These forms and topics are all practised in this book.)

When marking Question 5, based on the optional set book, examiners want to see if candidates have read and appreciated the set book and can show this through discussion and description of the book, using examples. Candidates are expected to have understood the book, though extensive literary interpretation of the book is not expected.

How do 'good' writers write?

1 When students have drawn up their diagrams, discuss them together as a class. Point out that there is not a strict linear progression through these nine stages; the writer will move backwards and forwards between the stages.

KEY   How do 'good' writers write?

1 *Sample answer:*

having an idea you want to write about

identifying the target reader

getting your ideas together

making notes on the topic

making a rough outline or plan

checking the reader will be interested

writing a first draft

revising and redrafting the article

writing out a neat copy ready for publishing

---

2 There are various answers to the second exercise, but here is a general guide:

C: very carefully planned; P: planned; U: completely unplanned
birthday card to a friend *P/U*
letter to your American penfriend *C/P*
postcard to your family *P/U*
short story *C*
note to a close friend *P/U*
letter applying for a job in Australia *C*
notes for a speech at a wedding *C/P*
English exam composition: 'Things I like to do' *C*
letter of complaint to a mail order company *P/C*
note to pin to your door while you go out *P*
love letter *C/P*

3 Put students in small groups to do the final task. Have a feedback session to compare their ideas. Draw students' attention to the note on planning.

How can I evaluate and improve my work?

Follow the first activity with a brief class round-up of ideas. Do students see marking and correction of their work simply as **corrective**? Or do they think it can have a **positive** role too, helping them improve and revise their work? Do they think the old saying 'You learn from your mistakes' is true? Do they think they can learn something from the process of reaching a correct version, or do they think they learn more from only studying correct English?

This book is organised on the principle that students can learn from the revision and reviewing stage of writing. Collaboration between students, discussion of their work with their colleagues and with you can help them not only produce a better, more polished piece of work this time but also help them produce better work in the future. They will also become more aware of how to assess their own written work and, therefore, how to improve upon it. The book aims to support and guide students through the whole process of writing – not just set them written tasks and then tell them how good or bad their answers are.

The correction code given here is for reference for both you and the students. We suggest that all marking of students' written work is done using this code (or a similar one you may prefer) to enable students to work out their own errors and correct them, and to give them a better idea of what their weakest areas are. (For instance, a piece of work returned to a student, covered in red pen is very demoralising, but if many of the correction code symbols marked in the text are the same, the student knows what area is causing a problem and can do something about improving it.)

It is important to remember not to swamp students' work continually with masses of red ink. The psychological effect of this can be devastating. Remember to praise good work as well as criticising bad work. A useful source on different methods of managing mistakes is *Correction* by Bartram and Walton (LTP 1991).

Correction code

Symbol	Meaning	Wrong	Right
Sp	spelling	tabel	table
P	punctuation/capitals	i speak english	I speak English
T	verb/tense	He come yesterday.	He came yesterday
N	number	She watch TV.	She watches TV
F	form	This book is bored.	This book is boring
WO	word order	I like very much eggs.	I like eggs very much
WW	wrong word	Today it's shiny.	Today it's sunny.
G	grammar	He doesn't listened.	He doesn't listen
A	article	He's at the work.	He's at work.
λ	omission	He tall.	He is tall
/	word too many	It's the his book.	It's the book/It's his book.
//	paragraphing		
N/A	not appropriate; wrong register	Dear Sir/Madam, Send me information	Dear Sir/Madam I would be grateful if you would send me some information
?	don't understand		
~~	not quite right		
✓	good		

Unit 1 **A funny thing happened**

You may wish to omit the review of past tenses and deal with them separately in other classes. Alternatively it may be a useful diagnostic exercise. This unit, like all other units, can, if necessary, be shortened by asking students to do the second planning activity for homework along with the task.

Preview

The preview section of a unit provides a very brief activity to arouse students' interest in the topic. Not all units have preview sections as in some cases the planning activity also fulfils the preview function.

Explain the task. Put students in pairs to discuss the various subjects. Have feedback on any particularly interesting stories.

Planning 1

Preteach any key vocabulary you think students will not be able to guess. Students should read the text individually and then do the exercise in pairs.

KEY   Planning 1

1 The middle four paragraphs tell the story.

2 1 We had been staying on Boracay.
    2 We booked a flight.
    3 We met the other passengers.
    4 We went to the airstrip.
    5 The pilot arrived.
    6 The plane took off.
    7 The pilot spoke on the radio.
    8 The transmission failed.
    9 We landed at Manila.

Draw students' attention to Exam Tip 1. A flow diagram is a useful way of jotting down random ideas, and arranging them in order, before beginning to write. It is particularly good for planning a **sequence** of events. In these exercises, students have done the process in reverse, going from text to diagram. Later in the unit they will have practice in using a flow diagram as a planning activity – going from diagram to text.

KEY Planning 1

3 The paragraphs in the text are as follows:
Paragraph 1: background
Paragraph 2: first events
Paragraph 3: later events
Paragraph 4: final events and outcome

Point out to students that this order is a good way of structuring a piece of narrative writing.

Working with the whole class, see if students can give examples of these four stages in just very short stories. Look at Exam Tip 2.

e.g. I was walking along the street on my way to work (*background*) when a dog ran in front of me (*first events*). I was watching the dog (*later events*) and stepped into a huge puddle (*final events and outcome*).

Past tenses

The purpose of these exercises is to raise students' awareness of the use of past tenses in narrative compositions. Teachers can give further practice in any or all of these tenses at a later date if necessary. Students can work in pairs or alone to complete these tasks.

KEY Past tenses

1

Past simple	d	We walked along the beach . . .
Past continuous	a	. . . the plane was already waiting.
Past perfect	b	We had just spent three weeks . . .
Past perfect continuous	c	. . . we had been renting a bamboo hut . . .

2 was   were walking   (had) started   had been going   came
had been able   had spent   could   stopped   made   had left

---

Time linking words

KEY   Time linking words

1 before   then   When   After a short time
quite soon afterwards   At first   after   as   Finally
while   Suddenly   Eventually   a few minutes later
in a few months

Have a feedback session and check that students have a complete list of
the time linking words in the text. If necessary, explain the meaning of
words. Students can now work in pairs to cross out the incorrect words
and phrases.

KEY   Time linking words

2 *Possible answers:*

1 when/as
2 suddenly
3 At first
4 then/quite soon afterwards
5 eventually/finally

6 A few minutes later/Quite
   soon afterwards
7 as/while/when
8 After/When
9 when

Planning 2

If necessary, help students to get started by asking a few general
questions about the pictures. What is a bicycle pump used for? What
sort of things can go wrong with bikes? Why might the flowers be
important? What could the cat have done?

Students should work in pairs and make up a story which involves all
the items pictured. Remind them of the four stages discussed earlier:
background, first events, later events, final events and outcome.

Still working in pairs, students should then organise the main events of
their story into a flow diagram. Afterwards, have a class feedback
session to compare different stories. You could also discuss whether they
found the flow diagrams a useful way of getting their ideas organised
into a sequential order, and find out if students use any other techniques
to order a sequence of ideas.

Exam question (narrative)

You can set the task for homework, or allow time for it in class. In
either case, encourage students to use the plans they worked out in
'Planning 2' to help them with the task.

Improving your work

The improving stage of each unit follows the writing task. These sections contain short activities designed to help students improve their writing by making them think about the techniques and processes they adopt when they write. Sections later in the book will deal with specific techniques that will be useful for the First Certificate.

Checking and polishing

It is important that you make time for checking and polishing after each writing task, either by allowing class time for it, or by setting it as a homework task.

Draw students' attention to Study Tip 1. Writing out a neat copy can help them revise and improve their work. It also means they have two versions on file to look back at later for revision purposes, to see where they made mistakes and how they corrected them, and it means that any corrections they made are clearly legible. Remember to use a clear correction code when marking (see page 8).

Unit 2 **On the road**

If you have already dealt with giving advice, or you intend to deal with it later separately, you may wish to omit the 'Giving advice' section. Alternatively it may be a useful diagnostic activity, or provide valuable extra practice. If you are short of time, the passage to punctuate at the end of 'Punctuating correctly' and the second planning activity can be done as homework.

Preview

This preview section is designed to arouse students' interest in the topic of travel in a light-hearted way. Get students to complete the questionnaire individually and then compare their answers in pairs.

A feedback discussion might just elicit which student scored the most points (and is therefore the best traveller!). Alternatively (or in addition) students could discuss why the (b) answers get the most points. If you want to extend the activity, you can ask students to write two or three more similar multiple choice questions.

Planning 1

It is probably best to elicit one or two ideas from the class as a whole first on one topic, e.g. health – *What are the main health precautions I will need to take? What vaccinations will I need to have?*, etc. Then, when students are clear about what they have to do, put them in pairs to make a list of further questions.

Have a class feedback session and make a list of all their questions on the board.

Point out to students that listing questions is often a good way of collecting ideas before they start any writing task (see Exam Tip 3).

Giving advice

1 Check that students are familiar with the advice structures before setting the exercise. Students can work out answers together in pairs or write down their answers individually. In either case a feedback session will be necessary to check their work.

KEY   Giving advice

1

Suggestions	Strong advice
Why not . . .? Why don't you . . . ? It might be a good idea to . . .	You'd better . . . You really should . . . You ought to . . . If I were you, I'd . . .

2 *Possible answers:*

You really should have a (valid) passport.
You ought to get the necessary visas.
It might be a good idea to take plenty of/enough money.
You'd better make sure you have the right vaccinations.
Why not take some protection against mosquitoes?
You ought to take a map.
You ought to take some T-shirts.
If I were you, I'd take some shorts.
It might be a good idea to take a sweater.
Why don't you take a Swahili phrasebook?
You should take out insurance.

Punctuating correctly

1 Elicit answers for the *Name* column from the class as a whole first. Students can then work on correcting the examples in pairs. Go through the answers with the class.

2 Students can do the second exercise individually. If there is not enough time in class for this, it can be set as extra homework. On the other hand, you may feel that punctuation is not a major problem. If this is the case, you may prefer to omit the exercise altogether.

Key ⇒

KEY Punctuating correctly

1

Feature	Name	Use	Example
A B C	capital letters	to start sentences	We need a visa to go there.
		for names	Tunisia and Algeria
		with 'I'	Tomorrow I leave for Egypt.
.	full stop	to end sentences	Travelling by train is cheap.
,	comma	to separate items in a list (but not before 'and')	cholera, malaria, polio and typhoid
		to add information	You must see the River Nile, which flows through Egypt.
:	colon	to start a list	Take a mixture of currency: £ sterling, French francs and US dollars.
		to add an explanation	Avoid drinking unboiled water: it is a major source of disease.
;	semi-colon	to separate items in lists of phrases	So remember what you need: lots of money; the right vaccinations; the right visas.
,	apostrophe	to show letters left out	You'll need a vaccination certificate.
		to indicate possession	The traveller's main problem is time.

2 *Possible answer:*

You should take clothes for hot and cold climates: (*or* climates. The) the desert, even though it's in Africa, gets very cold at night. In addition, don't forget the small essentials: water-purifying tablets; a needle and cotton; a pair of sunglasses; and one or two good books. I also take a penknife, a sleeping bag and a stove.

Draw students' attention to Exam Tip 4 and remind them that correct punctuation is important.

Planning 2

This planning exercise uses the technique practised in 'Planning 1' in the context of an exam question. You may wish to draw students' attention at this point to the exam question.

Students can do this planning exercise either in pairs or individually. In either case it would be useful to have a feedback session in which they compare their lists with each other. They will in this way be able to extend their lists before the final writing stage.

Remind students that they will have to order their ideas before writing their compositions. You can draw their attention to the earlier ordering exercise in Unit 1 for this.

There is a brief look at the layout of informal letters here. This is looked at in more detail in Unit 3 where it is contrasted with the layout of formal letters. Ask students to do the exercise by referring to the picture. Then check their answers.

Note that in the exam there are <u>no</u> marks given or deducted for including or omitting addresses on letters. In fact, candidates are specifically told on the exam paper not to include addresses in their letters. However, candidates are expected to know other conventions of letter writing: opening salutations, paragraphing, closing phrases, etc. (and in the real world they will need to know how to write addresses).

KEY Planning 2

1 false	3 false	5 true
2 true	4 false	6 false

Exam question (informal letter)

You can set this for homework, or allow time in class. Remind students to use the advice structures they have practised and to be careful with their punctuation.

Improving your work

Checking and polishing

Students work in pairs to polish their work. Allow class time or homework time for this. Remember to use a clear correction code when marking (see page 8).

Self-assessment 1

If you have marked students' work using the correction code (see page 8), it is easy for students to count up the symbols on their letter and assess their work.

Students should be encouraged to evaluate their own work and assess where their weaknesses lie. Having pinpointed these weaknesses, you should encourage students to do further remedial work on their own. Some possible areas for assessment are given in the Student's Book. Other areas are: register, paragraphing, handwriting, relevance, word order, clarity. Refer students back to the Foundation unit (pages 5, 6 and 7) if they have difficulty adding to the list in the table.

Ellis & Sinclair[1] suggest that students set themselves realistic short-term aims in order to manage their remedial work and see their progress. Students might draw up a chart of what they need to improve, how they could practise this, when they do it, etc. and then tick it off when they have fulfilled their aim, e.g.

What?	*How?*	*When?*	*How long?*	*Done*
Improve spelling	Copy out mistakes 3 times then test myself on them	by Friday	10 mins	✓
Improve vocab of sports	Read sports pages in newspapers	by Sunday	25 mins	✓

[1] *Learning to Learn English*, Gail Ellis and Barbara Sinclair (© CUP, 1989)

Unit 3 Learn a language

If you feel students are familiar with requests, or if you wish to deal with them separately later, you may wish to omit 'Making requests'. Alternatively it may provide a helpful diagnostic activity, or useful extra practice. If you are short of time, students can do the second planning exercise for homework along with the exam question.

Preview / Planning 1

'Brainstorming'

Find out if any of the class have been to Britain or any other country for a language course. If someone has, ask them to talk briefly about their experience.

If this is unlikely, ask students to speculate on the advantages and disadvantages of learning English in a native-speaker environment. Discuss what problems students might have.

Explain the idea of 'brainstorming' – that it is a method used to generate ideas, however bizarre they may seem at the time. Evaluation of the ideas is not part of the process of 'brainstorming'; that comes later.

Allow students five minutes in pairs; then put pairs together for a few minutes to compare answers and extend their lists.

Have a feedback session to collect together ideas from the class. Be careful not to be judgemental until all the ideas have been collected in.

Draw students' attention to Exam Tip 5, pointing out that 'brainstorming' is a useful activity before any composition.

Letter-writing rules

Laying out a letter

Point out that although students may be familiar with letter-writing conventions in their own language, they are not necessarily the same in English. They are not, however, particularly difficult; and they are something which students can guarantee to get right in an exam.

Ask students to read through the two letters, noting which of the ideas they came up with in **Planning 1** are mentioned in the letters. Ask one or two general comprehension questions about each letter before getting students to do the exercise.

Note that in the exam there are <u>no</u> marks given or deducted for including or omitting addresses on letters. In fact, candidates are specifically told on the exam paper not to include addresses in their letters. However, candidates are expected to know other conventions of letter writing: opening salutations, paragraphing, closing phrases, etc. (and in the real world they will need to know how to write addresses).

Go through the answers and draw students' attention to Exam Tip 6. They will probably need to refer back to this unit when writing other formal letters.

KEY Letter-writing rules: Laying out a letter			
	Informal letters	*Formal letters*	*Neither*
You usually begin Dear . . .	✓	✓	
You put your name in the top right-hand corner.			✓
You put your address in the top right-hand corner.	✓	✓	
You need not put your full address.	✓		
You should put the date under your address.	✓	✓	
You write the name and address of the person you are writing to in the top left-hand corner.		✓	
You do not put paragraphs.			✓
You can finish **Yours sincerely / Yours faithfully.**		✓	
You always use the first name of the person you are writing to.	✓		
You can sign your full name.		✓	
You can finish **Best wishes / Love from.**	✓		
You should put your name under your signature.		✓	
You can use contractions (e.g. I'd, I'll, etc.).	✓		

Starting and finishing a letter

Ask students to work in pairs filling in the table. Go through the answers and elicit any other beginnings and endings that students know, e.g. Dearest, Yours, All the best, etc.

Point out that it is important to use **Yours faithfully** with **Dear Sir or Madam,** etc. and **Yours sincerely** with **Dear Mr/Mrs/Ms/Miss Brown,** etc. It will count against them if they do not.

KEY   **Letter-writing rules:** Starting and finishing a letter

	Starting		*Finishing*
Intimate	Darling	→	Lots of love and kisses
Family	Dear Uncle Jim	→	Love from
Friendly	Dear Alice	→	Best wishes
Formal I	Dear Ms Cooper	→	Yours sincerely
Formal II	Dear Sir or Madam	→	Yours faithfully

Making requests

1 Students should do the first exercise on their own, then compare their answers with a partner and add to the list of request structures from their own experience. If they do not come up with any new ones, you may wish to introduce some or all of the following:

Would you . . . ?
Do you mind . . . ?
Would you mind . . . ?
Do you think you could . . . ?
Could you possibly . . . ?
I was wondering if you could . . . ?
I don't suppose you could . . . , could you?
You wouldn't be able to . . . , would you?

KEY   **Making requests**

1 *Possible answers:*

Friendly	Will you . . . ? / Can you . . . ?
Polite	Do you think you could . . . ? / I'd really appreciate it if you . . . / Please could you . . . ?
Formal	I would be grateful if you could . . . / I would appreciate it if you could . . .

---

2 Discuss with students what factors influence the choice of formality: the relationship between the speakers, the age of the speakers, the nature of the request, the setting, and so on. Point out the more formal request in the informal letter (for a more time-consuming request), and the less formal, but nonetheless polite, request in the formal letter (for a more straightforward request).

3 Put students in small groups or pairs for the next exercise. Allow them time to work out the answers. Then check the answers round the class.

Planning 2

This time students should do the 'brainstorming' activity on their own first, before progressing in pairs to compare and extend their notes. If there is time, ask students to start making a rough plan for their composition.

Exam question (formal letter)

You can set this for homework or allow time in class. Remind students to lay out their letters correctly and to try and use the request structures practised earlier, concentrating on getting the right level of formality.

Improving your work

Checking and polishing

Students work in pairs to polish their work. Allow class time or homework time for this. Remember to use a clear correction code when marking (see page 8).

Organising your work

Ask students to complete the questionnaire. Hold a class discussion, encouraging students to take up some of the ideas for organising their work and suggest ways in which they might do so, e.g. cutting out articles from newspapers, having a penfriend, etc. Draw students' attention to Study Tip 3.

Unit 4 **A tall, dark, handsome stranger**

If you feel students are familiar with the vocabulary and structures in 'Adjectives for describing people' you may wish to omit this section. Alternatively you may wish to deal with it later separately. If you are short of time, the second planning activity can be done as homework along with the exam question.

Preview

When students have speculated on the photos for a few minutes, have a feedback session comparing the views of different pairs. Then ask students to close their books and try and describe the people in the photos.

Another useful preview exercise is 'Back-to-back' from *Drama Techniques in Language Learning* by Maley and Duff (© CUP, 1982).

Planning 1

Explain that a 'spidergraph' is for organising information into groups, for instance, to group all the information about appearance together, all the ideas about character together, and so on. This helps to avoid producing a jumbled and disorganised set of disjointed facts. It also helps avoid having a single, 'floating' idea or sentence that does not really fit into the general structure. It also helps to plan paragraphs. It is more useful here than a flow diagram, because the subject of the written task is not narrative/sequential in nature. Put students into pairs to complete the 'spidergraph', giving help where necessary. Draw students' attention to Exam Tip 7.

Key ➡

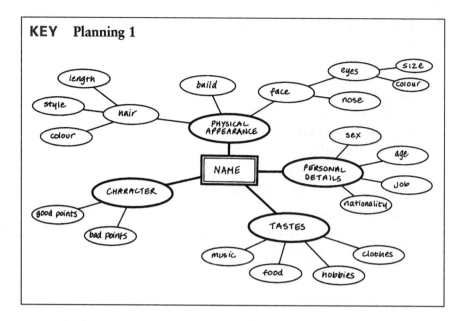

KEY   Planning 1

Adjectives for describing people

1 Explain that students should decide on their own criteria for sorting the adjectives. Encourage them to ask each other or use dictionaries to find out the meanings of any words they do not know.

> **KEY   Adjectives for describing people**
>
> **1** *One possible grouping is:*
>
> fair   wavy   curly   blond   dark
> (*words used to describe hair*)
>
> short   plump   slim   tall   thin
> (*words used to describe build*)
>
> honest   friendly   independent   shy   generous
> stubborn
> (*words used to describe character*)
>
> handsome   smart   scruffy   attractive
> (*words used to describe general appearance*)

2 Words that might be considered negative or critical are: *shy, stubborn, scruffy*. There may be some discussion about these. For example, not everyone may consider *shy* to be negative; some people may find other adjectives contain a negative connotation. Let the discussion happen.

3 Ask students to use the box to make sentences about the people in the Preview activity above.

If necessary, remind students that generally:

looks + adjective
looks like + noun
looks as if + clause

Once students have got the idea you can give them further practice with magazine pictures.

KEY   Adjectives for describing people

3 looks + attractive/honest
  looks like + a film star/a boxer
  looks as if + she's friendly/he's had a bad day

Ordering adjectives

1 This exercise is designed to check that the students know the different types of adjectives.

2 Put students in pairs to look at the second exercise. By studying the phrases they should be able to work out the usual order for the different types of adjectives.

Stress that students are very unlikely to come across more than three adjectives together, and that one (or two) is the norm.

3 Set the last exercise for homework if time is short; or leave it out if the order of adjectives is not a problem for your class.

KEY   Ordering adjectives

1 colour – blue   age – old
  material – wooden   origin – Italian
  size – large   shape – round
  opinion – wonderful

2 1 opinion   3 age   5 colour   7 material
  2 size   4 shape   6 origin

3 a) a stylish blue Armani jacket   d) an ugly large red nose
  b) a fashionable short leather skirt e) small black leather shoes
  c) attractive short brown hair   f) large round blue eyes

Planning 2

Get students to draw their 'spidergraphs' on their own. Give them time to compare their efforts with other students in the class so that they can incorporate ideas from other people.

Exam question (description)

You can set this for homework or allow time in class. Remind students to use their 'spidergraph' plan to help them, and to use some of the adjectives they have learned.

Improving your work

Checking and polishing

Students work in pairs to polish their work. Allow class time or homework time for this. Remember to use a clear correction code when marking (see page 8).

Adding interest and personalisation

1 Whilst you should encourage students to express (and explain) their own preferences, point out that to an examiner, passage 1 is much better.

Help students to work out what makes passage 1 more interesting.

2 Students should bear the points discussed in 1 in mind when rewriting the last passage. Draw students' attention to Exam Tip 8.

Key ➡

KEY Improving your work: Adding interest and personalisation

1 Using longer words does not necessarily make a text more interesting.

Using a wide variety of adjectives definitely improves a text. Passage 2 uses only *tall, slim* and *nice*; passage 1 uses *bossy, amusing, adventurous* and *responsible* which succeed in telling the reader much more exactly what the writer likes about his/her brother and their relationship.

Using longer sentences can help to improve the interest of a text. Strings of short, simple sentences are abrupt and disjointed to read. Longer sentences with ideas linked together make easier and more interesting reading.

Giving details rather than just general, vague information makes a text more interesting – the writer of passage 1 tells us exactly what he/she likes about the brother and what hobbies they share, whereas the writer of passage 2 just says *we go out together to lots of different places* and *we go on holiday together* and does not engage the reader's interest.

Telling the reader what you think makes a text more personal, and therefore more interesting. It makes a text seem real. In passage 1 the writer tells us how he/she feels about the brother, whereas in passage 2 we have no idea.

A text is not necessarily interesting just because it is long. If students read over their work and it seems boring, they should try following the points mentioned above to improve it – making it longer doesn't help at all!

Unit 5 Through the grapevine

Preview

This is a walk-round activity to encourage students to think about the topic of the media. Have a brief feedback session to find out any points of interest – students who have been in the papers, etc.

Planning 1

Put students in pairs to do this exercise. When the pairs have done as much as they can, have a feedback session and pool the ideas from the whole class. Make sure everyone adds other ideas to their lists during this activity.

Paragraphing

Ask students to predict, on the basis of their discussion in Planning 1, what sort of vocabulary they would expect to find in a composition discussing the advantages and disadvantages of pocket televisions. Write their ideas on the board and teach any vocabulary they are unlikely to know, e.g. *benefit, drawback, screen, convenient, convenience.*

For a pre-task activity, ask students to read through the paragraphs quickly and see how many of their own ideas have been mentioned.

Then get students to read the paragraphs more carefully and do the task in pairs.

KEY **Paragraphing**

Para 1 – B – introduction   Para 3 – A – advantages
Para 2 – D – disadvantages   Para 4 – C – opinion

Emphasise that this is a good way of structuring a discussion essay. Point out that it is equally possible to organise a composition as follows: introduction, advantages, disadvantages, opinion. The important thing is that there is a clear beginning and a clear ending and that the advantages and disadvantages are kept separate and not muddled up.

Talking about advantages and disadvantages

Make sure students have a record of these expressions for future reference. (Note that there are some useful linking words in the composition given here – these are dealt with in other units.)

KEY	Talking about advantages and disadvantages	
A major A further One	advantage benefit good thing	is . . .
One further Another Another major	problem drawback disadvantage	

Put students in groups for the second exercise. If there is time, have a feedback session and pool ideas.

Planning 2

If time is short, students can do this for homework. First make sure that students know what censorship is. Discuss when/where/how it works. Get them to make lists on their own first. Then allow them to compare their answers and expand their lists in preparation for the exam question below.

Exam question (discussion essay)

You can set this for homework or allow time in class. Remind students of the composition structure in 'Paragraphing' and the language items in 'Talking about advantages and disadvantages'. Encourage them to use these as much as possible.

Improving your work

Checking and polishing

Students work in pairs to polish their work. Allow class time or homework time for this. Remember to use the correction code when marking (see page 8).

What we write

Students fill in the table on their own, adding as many items as they can. Put them in pairs to compare their answers then have a feedback session. Try and increase students' awareness of the kinds of texts they write. Elicit from students the differences between different types of text (layout, level of formality, length, etc.). Encourage students to think about what types of writing they need for the FCE exam and also what other kinds of writing in English they might need.

Unit 6 Being green

If time is short, the second planning activity can be done for homework, as can the second exercise in 'Linking words for reason and result'.

Preview

A good introduction to this unit would be to open a short discussion on a particular local environmental issue, eliciting the opinions of as many students as possible. Alternatively, you could 'brainstorm' and open up discussion of 'green' issues in general.

Put students in pairs to work out and group the anagrams.

KEY Preview

Sources of power: electricity   gas   nuclear power   coal   wind
Things that can be recycled: glass   paper   aluminium   tyres   batteries
Endangered animals: panda   gorilla   leopard   rhinoceros   whale

---

Planning 1

Allow students time to complete the questionnaire and fill in their opinions, then put them in pairs to compare opinions with their partner. Some suggestions for topics which could be added to the questionnaire: use of animals to test medicine, vegetarianism, fur coats, leaded petrol, recycling, renewable power sources, irradiation of food, organic food, etc.

If students are prone to mistakes such as *'I'm agree' or overuse of 'Yes, but . . .' as a method of disagreement, draw their attention to the box before they start discussing the questionnaire.

As the questions are fairly wide-ranging, discussion may well start on any number of issues. Encourage the discussion to continue. If there is time, have a feedback session focusing on points of particular interest and on important vocabulary.

Draw students' attention to Exam Tip 11. Often one of the biggest problems with writing is having enough ideas. An exercise like this is designed to help them think of ideas for themselves. It may be worth drawing their attention to the variety of questions that they have written themselves in the first three sections of the questionnaire and especially in the Food section, where they have had no help at all.

Evaluating information and layout

Introduce the situation with books closed and ask students to speculate on what plans the council might have come up with for spending the money. Build up a list of possibilities and introduce any relevant vocabulary.

Point out that students may be required to exercise their judgement regarding certain information and to back their judgement up with argument and reasoning. There will not necessarily be a 'right' or 'wrong' answer. Students may be daunted by the amount of material in this section. Point out that the tasks they have to perform are actually quite straightforward and they need not worry unduly.

1 Allow students time to read the information and evaluate the different plans on the grid provided. Then put them in pairs to compare their ideas. It is important to allow class discussion at this point so that students can clarify their thoughts and express their reasons. Point out that this is the process they will have to go through in the exam – albeit rather more quickly and by themselves.

2 Put students in pairs to compare the layouts of the three different reports. Have a follow-up discussion and draw out the following points:
  – The environmental report gives little information and is not very clearly laid out.
  – The charity report, although short, is quite clearly argued and the bullet points make it clear what the money will be spent on.
  – The transport report is very full and clearly paragraphed; each paragraph is clearly headed; and it is clear what the recommendation is. This is the best layout.

Linking words for reason and result

Give students time to read through the articles again and underline the linkers.

KEY **Linking words for reason and result**

1 *Linking words to underline:*
Because so that As a result Since As therefore so

2 *Linking words for gaps:*
  1 because/as/since   2 as a result/therefore   3 as/because/since
  4 therefore   5 so   6 so that   7 therefore

---

3 Now ask students to read through the Budget Committee report again and say whether they agree or disagree with it, giving reasons.

Planning 2

Go through the exam question with the class and elicit one or two questions that they might consider. For example:

What age range would the leisure centre cater for?
How expensive would the old people's accommodation be?

Put students into pairs to compare their answers. Alternatively have a class feedback session, pooling ideas on the board. Point out to students that this is the process they will have to go through on their own in the exam.

Exam question (report)

You can set this for homework or allow time in class. Remind students to think about the layout of their report and the correct use of linkers of reason and result. Remind them also of the word limit.

Improving your work

Checking and polishing

Students work in pairs to polish their work. Allow class time or homework time for this. Remember to use a clear correction code when marking (see page 8).

Why we write

Students fill in the table on their own adding as many items as they can. Put them in pairs to compare their answers and have a feedback session. Try and increase students' awareness of the reasons why they write – both in their own language and in English. Elicit from them how the reason for writing will influence the type of language used – the language in a letter inviting a friend to stay will be different from that in a letter apologising to a friend for forgetting a dinner invitation. Encourage students to think about how writing 'in order to pass the First Certificate' will affect the way they write.

Unit 7 **Work to live!**

Preview/Planning 1

Before students open their books, you could elicit from them what kind of things they think are important when choosing a job. When they have come up with a few ideas, get them to open their books and do the planning activity individually. They can then compare their answers in pairs.

Point out that ranking ideas, numbering them in order of priority, is a very simple but effective planning technique when writing. Random ideas, roughly jotted down can be turned into a sound writing plan simply by thinking about them for a while and numbering them in order before beginning to write.

Selecting relevant information

This task deals with a skill that students may well need for the compulsory question in Part 1 of the Writing paper. It is important that students learn to work out which information is relevant and which can be ignored. Working alone, students should fill in the table. When they have finished, have a class round-up to compare and check answers.

Key ➡

KEY   Selecting relevant information

job	qualifications/ experience/ skills needed	duties	training given	hours	pay	contact
A NURSERY COOK	*recognised craft quals. preferred*	*cooking for 100 children*	*full training given*	*Mon–Fri 7.30am– 3pm*	*£4.75 per hour*	*Head Office 01180 147676*
B SALES PEOPLE	*aged 23–45*	*selling*	*full training & support*		*£25–40K pa*	*Thomas Adams on 0800 09981*
C SHOP FLOOR CLEANERS		*cleaning shop floors*	*yes*	*Mon–Sat 7–9am; 4 days a week 5–7pm*	*£5 per hour*	*M. Harris on 0112 052413*
D STORE DETECTIVES	*experience needed*	*looking after retail clients*		*40–45 hours per week*	*£5.50–£6 per hour*	*Personnel Dept. on 0113 0407603*
E PART-TIME REC/ TYPIST/ CLERK	*computer literate & Word Perfect experience*	*receptionist typist clerk*		*to be agreed*		*Mrs M. Clarke*
F AU PAIR/ NANNY		*looking after two boys, aged 1 and 3*		*8am–6pm*		*Ring Jane on 0119 0249121*
G	*enthusiasm, aged 21+*	*driving a BMW*			*£500 per week*	*Ring 0991 060606*

Students should look back at the information in the advertisements that they have not underlined and decide how relevant it is to job seekers. Refer students to Exam Tip 16.

Give students a few moments to think about which job appeals to them. Let them discuss their decision in pairs or elicit opinions round the class; make sure students give reasons for their answers.

Interpreting abbreviations

It is quite possible that students will need to understand abbreviations – especially in the compulsory task in Part 1. Students should be familiar with some of the more common abbreviations, and should have experience at working out others. A list of abbreviations can be found at the back of the *Macmillan Student's Dictionary* and in most other dictionaries.

1 The first exercise gives examples of eight abbreviations in context for students to try and work out. Get students to do the exercise in pairs and help each other.

KEY Interpreting abbreviations

1 a) in the morning b) in the afternoon/evening c) curriculum vitae
d) Monday e) Friday f) thousand g) per year (per annum)
h) as soon as possible

---

2 The second exercise is uncontextualised but provides a list of twelve very common abbreviations that students should know.

KEY Interpreting abbreviations

2 a) for example b) telephone c) please reply
d) Member of Parliament e) Bachelor of Arts (or possibly
British Airways or Buenos Aires) f) especially g) kilometre(s)
h) postscript i) please note j) title before a woman's name
k) or near offer (this means a seller will accept an offer close to the
asking price) l) kilogram

Planning 2

To help them answer the question, students should first underline the information in the letter and then in the job advertisements.

KEY   Planning 2

Dear Sir/Madam,

After <u>two and a half years as secretary to the Publishing Director of The Butterfield Press, I am now looking for a new post</u> in which I can develop my skills further. I am, therefore, writing to you to inquire if you know of any job opportunities which might suit me.

<u>The post at the Butterfield Press was my first job after leaving university.</u> While working there, <u>I have developed very good word processing skills including audio typing. I have also been involved in dealing directly with authors, organising seminars and taking considerable responsibility for a number of public functions.</u>

<u>I am looking for a challenging post that will further develop my skills. I would also like an increase on my current salary of £12,500 pa.</u>

I look forward to hearing from you.

Yours faithfully,

Amanda Forrest

Amanda Forrest

Exam question (formal letter)

This task can be done in class or for homework. Remind students to use appropriate information when recommending a job to Amanda.

Improving your work

Checking and polishing

Students work in pairs to polish their work. Allow class time or homework time for this. Remember to use a clear correction code when marking (see page 8).

Clear handwriting

Stress to students that neat handwriting and clear correction of their work is essential for good exam results. Draw attention to Exam Tip 18.

- The examiners can only give marks for what they can actually read! Remember they have several hundred scripts to mark.
- Tidy and clear work gives a better general impression – the examiner is more likely to be kindly disposed towards you!
- Untidy work gives an impression of the student not having put much effort into the work – even if this is not true!
- It is more difficult for examiners to follow the thread of what you are saying in your answer if they have to struggle to read it.

In classwork, students should be encouraged to make a neat, final copy of their writing tasks. In the exam, shortage of time does not always make this possible, so it is worth giving students help to make sure their exam answers are clear and legible.

1 Help students improve their handwriting – give them extra tasks such as copying if their handwriting is very bad, particularly if they are struggling with a different alphabet and script from their own language.

2 Suggest that they devise a clear system for correcting their work, so it is obvious to an examiner what they have crossed out and what they have replaced it with. For instance, they could always cross out mistakes with a couple of bold lines and then write the correct version above. Or they could write the correct version in the margin, or below the crossing out. The important thing is to be consistent so that the examiner is not hunting all over the page trying to find out what students are trying to say. Writing on alternate lines is a good way of making sure students have plenty of room to write corrections in clearly.

3 A rough plan or brief first draft done before students start writing is the best way to cut down on the number of mistakes and corrections in their answer.

Unit 8 **Bestsellers**

If you feel students are familiar with the vocabulary and structures in
'Expressing attitude', or you want to deal with them later separately,
you may wish to omit this section. Alternatively it may be a helpful
diagnostic exercise or provide useful extra practice. If you are short of
time, students can do the second planning activity for homework as well
as the exam question.

Preview

This is one of the two units that also deals in part with the set book.
Obviously, as the set books change from year to year, it is impossible to
deal with specific questions that might arise. We do, however, look at
some areas of language that might be useful in answering the set book
questions.

This preview section encourages students to talk about their reading in
general.

Planning 1

Previous planning activities have been concerned with the generation of
ideas rather than deciding which ideas are suitable to be used. In this
unit we concern ourselves more with the selection of points.

Ask students to do the exercise on their own first and then compare
their answer with a partner.

KEY   **Planning 1**

One possible answer is to cross out the following:
– The book is 224 pages long.
– My sister likes reading too.
– The picture on the cover is striking.
– The blurb on the back is interesting.
– My friend Sue liked it.
– The author had written three books before this one.
– I've never been to Arizona.

Students may feel that some of these points should be included, or that
there are other points which should be omitted. If this is so, allow
discussion to develop with students justifying their points of view.

Organising an article (title and structure)

1 Give students time to read the article and choose which title they like best. Have a feedback session comparing answers and drawing out the following points: *a* and *b* are accurate but rather boring titles which are hardly likely to catch the reader's attention; *c* and *d* are much more interesting; *c* is more eyecatching and gives the reader an idea of the reviewer's opinion and *d* suggests that it is headline news. Either of these would be good titles.

Stress the importance of thinking of a good title for an article.

2 Students may need a few minutes to look again at the article before doing this exercise. Check answers with the class and stress that it is important that an article has a clear structure.

KEY Organising an article (title and structure)

2 1 – Introduction and background   4 – How the story develops
    2 – The hero   5 – Different elements of the
    3 – The beginning of the story   story
                                                     6 – The opinion of the reviewer

---

Expressing attitude

Put students in pairs to fill in the table. Go through the answers sorting out any language problems. Elicit from individual students one or two opinions similar to those in the speech bubbles before putting students in groups to discuss their literary tastes. Go round the class monitoring the groups and dealing with any language problems.

KEY Expressing attitude

amuse	amusing	delight	delightful
impress	impressive	fascinate	fascinating
interest	interesting	offend	offensive
excite	exciting	depress	depressing
thrill	thrilling	annoy	annoying
bore	boring	irritate	irritating
convince	convincing		

Planning 2

1 Remind students of 'brainstorming' and other techniques for generating ideas. Ask them to think of six to eight reasons why they like the book they have chosen. Stress that these reasons do not have to be entirely serious as the second part of the exercise will involve selecting relevant points.

2 When students have finished their own list, ask them to exchange lists with a partner and go through selecting the most relevant points.

Have a feedback session to discuss any problems that have arisen.

Exam question (article)

You can set this for homework or allow time in class. Remind students to think carefully about the title and structure of their article, and to remember different ways of expressing attitude.

Improving your work

Checking and polishing

Students work in pairs to polish their work. Allow class time or homework time for this. Remember to use a clear correction code when marking (see page 8).

Using resources

1 Work through this stage together with the class, discussing the ideas, encouraging the class to try and improve the way they organise their time and resources. Perhaps the class would like some class time to be set aside on a regular basis (perhaps twenty minutes once a fortnight, or ten minutes once a week) for them to review their recent work, look up new words in the dictionary, do quick revision exercises, etc. You can be on hand to answer questions or give explanations where students feel unsure about something.

Students need encouragement with general organisation, otherwise they start their exam revision and are faced with a chaotic, jumbled file of mixed notes, written work, and other pieces of paper, with no logical order or organisation – and an exam only a week away!

2 Encourage students to think of other resources they can exploit. Some possibilities might be: language labs, libraries, self-access centres, computers, English newspapers, cassettes, videos, music, English-language clubs, etc. Give students details of any English-language programmes, films, books, etc., that you know about by putting a notice on the board, or telling them about it at the start of a class.

Unit 9 **Family life**

Preview

Put students into small groups to discuss the quotations. Have a feedback session to exchange the ideas of different groups.

Planning 1

In Unit 5 students practised listing advantages and disadvantages in a discussion essay. The technique practised here is a mixture of that and a 'spidergraph' (see Unit 4). It has the advantage over list-making of not imposing any order initially. However, you should point out to students that once they have thought of and written down points using this technique they will need to order them in some way before starting to write their composition.

Make sure students compare their answers and add any ideas that they find they have missed. Draw their attention to Exam Tip 22.

Opening and closing paragraphs

If necessary refresh students' memory of the likely structure of a discussion essay (introduction, advantages, disadvantages, opinion/conclusion – see Unit 5). Elicit what sort of opening and closing paragraphs they would expect. Ask them to choose the best opening and closing paragraph, and decide what is wrong with the ones they do not choose.

Before you go through their answers, ask students to look at the lists of criteria for opening and closing paragraphs and decide which items are true. Then check their answers.

Key ➡

KEY   Opening and closing paragraphs

1 B would be the best opening: A gives an example; C expresses an opinion, which should come after consideration of the points for and against; D is waffly and tells the reader nothing; B gives some background information, limits the topic slightly (in the western world) and has none of the above faults.

2 C would be the best closing paragraph: A may be true but it is not a conclusion to a composition of this title – it sounds more like a piece of extra information added on as an afterthought; B seems to be part of the argument, not part of the conclusion; D is a personal opinion, but it is one which would be based on the conclusion of this composition; it also gives an example not a conclusion; C expresses the writer's opinion, rounds up the arguments and provides a satisfactory conclusion.

3 An opening paragraph should:
   – show there are two sides to a question
   – make a general comment on the subject
   – talk about what the question means

A closing paragraph should:
   – summarise the arguments very briefly in one or two sentences
   – state your own opinion
   – state any conclusions you reach

4 Get students to work in pairs producing opening and closing paragraphs. Go round the class helping and checking. Make sure students keep them so they can use them later. Point out that if they want to change them when they come to write their compositions, they may do so.

Recognising how a text links together

First get students to look back at their plans in 'Planning 1'. They should then read the text quickly to find out which of their ideas have been included. Then get them to look at and analyse the structure of the text, seeing how it compares with that in Unit 5.

Go through the first paragraph with the class explaining how forward and backward reference holds the text together, and which words are used to achieve this.

Put students in pairs to go through the rest of the text doing the same.

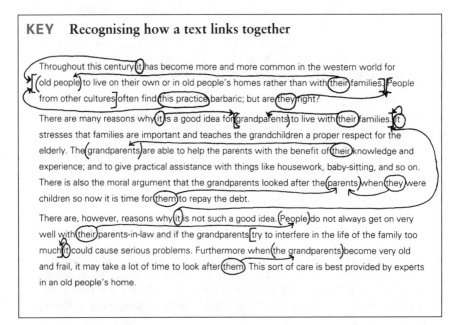

KEY   Recognising how a text links together

Throughout this century it has become more and more common in the western world for old people to live on their own or in old people's homes rather than with their families. People from other cultures often find this practice barbaric; but are they right?

There are many reasons why it is a good idea for grandparents to live with their families. It stresses that families are important and teaches the grandchildren a proper respect for the elderly. The grandparents are able to help the parents with the benefit of their knowledge and experience; and to give practical assistance with things like housework, baby-sitting, and so on. There is also the moral argument that the grandparents looked after the parents when they were children so now it is time for them to repay the debt.

There are, however, reasons why it is not such a good idea. People do not always get on very well with their parents-in-law and if the grandparents try to interfere in the life of the family too much it could cause serious problems. Furthermore when the grandparents become very old and frail, it may take a lot of time to look after them. This sort of care is best provided by experts in an old people's home.

Planning 2

If you are short of time, students can do this exercise for homework.

Ask students to repeat the planning exercise practised earlier. Put them in pairs to compare ideas and improve their plans. Then get them to order and number the points they have written down.

If students are by this time getting bored with the traditional, serious type of exam question, it is always possible to set a similar sort of question but with less serious content, or even allow students to make up their own questions (though some students do prefer guidance).

Examples of such questions (some student-generated, some teacher-generated) are:

- Discuss the advantages and disadvantages of having no hair.
- Discuss the advantages and disadvantages of colonisation in Africa.
- Discuss the advantages and disadvantages of choosing the title of a composition. (!)

Exam question (discussion essay)

You can set this for homework or allow time in class. Remind students to think carefully about their first and last sentences, and to pay attention to cohesion.

Improving your work

Checking and polishing

Students work in pairs to polish their work. Allow class time or homework time for this. Remember to use a clear correction code when marking (see page 8).

Learning useful expressions

Ask students to spend a few minutes looking at the list and reflecting on their own practice. Then let them compare ideas in pairs and groups. Have a feedback session and compare ideas from everyone in the class. Point out that there is no right and wrong way to learn words and expressions. Different methods work for different people. In general though a lot of exposure, written or aural, is a great help.

Suggest that everyone chooses a new technique to try out before the next lesson and that they choose half a dozen new words or expressions from this unit to remember. Get feedback at the beginning of the next lesson as to how successful this experiment has been and suggest that students again try out a new technique.

Unit 10 **Shop till you drop!**

Preview

With books closed, elicit from the class the names of different departments that they might find in a department store. Then get students to open their books and sort the vocabulary in the preview activity.

KEY	Preview

Books	Menswear	Electrical goods	China	Toys	Sports
an encyclopedia a travel guide a novel	a shirt a tie a sweater	a food processor a light bulb a toaster	a dish a bowl a vase	a doll a teddy bear a model boat	a shuttlecock a tennis racquet a rugby ball

Planning 1

1 With books closed elicit from the students the sort of features which make a shop popular and successful. Make a list on the board and then get students to open their books. Elicit one or two possible questions for the questionnaire and then let students work on more questions on their own.

2 Put students in pairs to choose a shop/shops to discuss and then ask and answer the questions they have devised.

The language and style of reports

This section gets students to look more closely at the language and style of reports. Draw their attention during the activities to the objective style that is generally used in reports.

1 Give students time to read through the report and pick out the inappropriately written paragraph. This is the 'Departments' paragraph, which is far too conversational/chatty in style.

2 Put students in pairs to rewrite the paragraph. Go round helping with language where necessary.

KEY   The language and style of reports

Possible answer:

2 Claridge's is a large store with a comprehensive range of departments (see list below). Surprisingly there is not a music department.

---

3 Students should then underline or note down any words and expressions which they think might be useful in future reports. Have a feedback session and pool the language that students have noted.

Linking words for concession and contrast

1 Ask students to look at the sentences from the report and circle the appropriate connectives.

KEY   Linking words for concession and contrast

1 Even though   Although   However   Despite

---

2 Point out the different grammar associated with each expression. 'Even though' and 'Although' are conjunctions; 'However' is an adverb; 'Despite' is a preposition. If necessary you could ask students to copy out the following tables:

The simple version

It was raining but we went out anyway.

The adverb versions (two sentences)

It was raining.	However, Nevertheless,	we went out anyway.

Key ⟶

45

The conjunction version (one sentence – two clauses)

Although Even though In spite of the fact (that) Despite the fact (that)	it was raining,	we went out.

The preposition version (one sentence – prepositional phrase)

Despite In spite of	the rain,	we went out.

3 Ask students to rewrite the sentences and to use a variety of different linkers when doing so.

4 This activity focuses on the grammar of these connectives – a feature which often causes students problems.

KEY   Linking words for concession and contrast

2 *Possible answers:*
   in spite of (the fact that)   nevertheless   despite the fact that   but

3 *Possible answers:*
   This is not the ideal location. However, it is close enough to the High Street to attract many casual shoppers.

   Despite the wide range of products, there is not a wide choice of brand names within each product.

   Although the electronics department, for example, sells every kind of device you could possibly want, there are only two different brands of television and three makes of cassette recorder.

   Even though there is only a narrow range of brand names, the quality is very high.

4 a Although the staff are generally polite, . . .
   b Even though credit cards are not accepted, . . .
   c There are stairs and escalators. However, there are . . .
   d correct
   e In spite of the smallness of the book department, . . .
   f The gift department is large but it is not . . .

Planning 2

Students should use ideas from Planning 1 as well as thinking of new ideas to list appropriate questions.

Exam question (report)

You can set this for homework or allow time in class. Remind students to concentrate on writing a report in the appropriate style and to be careful with the grammar of any connectives of concession that they use.

Improving your work

Checking and polishing

Students work in pairs to polish their work. Allow class time or homework time for this. Remember to use a clear correction code when marking (see page 8).

Self-assessment 2

1 Students should be encouraged to repeat the process they went through in Unit 2. You can then get them to compare their results with those in Unit 2 and ask students to reflect on which areas still need work and which areas they feel they have improved.

2 The second part of this section looks specifically at the FCE exam. Students have by now attempted at least one of each type of composition required by the exam. They can now indicate how confident they feel about each type. This will provide useful feedback as to where the emphasis should be placed in the run-up to the exam. It will also show you which areas you can encourage students to work on on their own.

Unit 11 **Jobhunting**

If you are short of time the 'Making applications' and 'Planning 2' activities can be set as homework as well as the exam question.

Preview

This is a short speaking exercise as a brief warmer to the topic of 'work'. Students work on their own and then compare their answers. Have a short feedback session to see which are generally the most appealing and the least appealing jobs of all in the list. Students may need some help with vocabulary: *stockbroker, confidence trickster.*

Planning 1

Students list and group their questions according to the instructions. If they have difficulty in grouping them you could prompt them with suggestions such as: personal details, education, experience, etc. Point out that some questions will be specific to the particular job, e.g. *experience with animals*, but that much information applies to all jobs. You could supplement these advertisements with real examples from local newspapers.

Paragraphing: recognising topic and illustrative sentences

1 Point out that this method of organising a paragraph (i.e. starting with a topic sentence to state the general theme and then expanding with examples and illustrative sentences) is a very common method of paragraph organisation in English. However, sometimes the topic sentence can come later in the paragraph, as in the second example given.

When students have completed the task, they will find the completed letter on page 70 of the Student's Book.

Key ➡

KEY   Paragraphing: recognising topic and illustrative sentences

1 *Topic sentence:* 'I was retiring after 29 years with the company'.

2

Paragraph	*Heading*	*Sentences*	*Topic Sentence*
B	Reason for writing	e d	e
E	Qualifications	o q p n	o
A	Experience	b a c	b
C	Languages	i g h f	i
D	Reason for application	j m k l	j

The completed letter of application should be as follows. Topic sentences are shown in bold type.

> 12 Priory Road
> Scarborough
> North Yorkshire
>
> 19th November 1999
>
> The Personnel Officer
> Angus Hotel Group
> 75–81 Sauchiehall St
> Glasgow
>
> Dear Sir or Madam,
>
> **I would like to apply for the post of Hotel Manager at the Glasgow Angus as advertised in this month's issue of 'The Caterer'.** As you will see from my c.v., I have the qualifications, experience and language proficiency you require.
>
> **I have both an external qualification and internal certificates from Fiesta Hotels.** Initially I obtained a diploma from the Hotel and Catering Institute of Management Association. In addition to that, I have attended a number of training courses run by Fiesta Hotels. These included ones on health and hygiene, fire prevention, and interviewing skills and techniques.
>
> **I have considerable experience in hotel management.** For the last five years I have been deputy manager at the Scarborough Fiesta. In previous posts I have worked in a wide variety of areas including housekeeping, reception, personnel and restaurant.
>
> **I speak three foreign languages well.** The first, French, I speak fluently, having lived in France for three years. I also speak good Spanish and some Italian. I feel this would be useful in a large international hotel which deals with clients from all over the world.

> There are a number of reasons for my applying for this post. First, having worked as a deputy manager for several years, I now feel ready to take on the challenge and responsibility of being a manager. Furthermore, I would like to work in a larger hotel with a more varied and international clientele. And finally I would also like to live and work in Glasgow – the city where I was brought up as a child and where most of my family and friends still live.
>
> I look forward to hearing from you.
>
> Yours faithfully
>
> *J. D. Ferguson*
>
> J. D. Ferguson

Draw students' attention to Exam Tip 26, pointing out that it is usual to keep separate types of information in different paragraphs in English. Thus a common structure for a letter of application will be: reason for writing, qualifications, experience, reasons for application. The extra paragraph in this letter about languages is specific to the job being applied for.

Making applications

By this stage students should be very familiar with the language of the letter, and this exercise should not take too much time. Encourage students to note down examples of formal written language that they will be able to transfer to other formal pieces of writing.

KEY   Making applications

Possible answers:

I would like to apply for the post of . . .
. . . as advertised in . . .
As you will see from my c.v. . . .
I obtained a diploma from . . .
In addition to that, I have attended (a number of) training courses . . .
I have considerable experience in . . .
In previous posts . . .
I have worked in a wide variety of areas . . .
I feel this would be useful in . . .
There are a number of reasons for my applying for this post.
I feel ready to take on the challenge and responsibility of . . .
I would like to work in . . .
I look forward to hearing from you.

Planning 2

Students should refer back to the questions they listed in 'Planning 1'. Using these questions they should note down the information needed to answer the exam question and organise this information into groups that can later be used as paragraphs.

Exam question (formal letter)

You can set this for homework or allow time in class. Remind students to look back at the organisation of paragraphs, the structure of paragraphs and the language used. If necessary, clarify that the guides will escort English-speaking tourists around the students' own local area.

Point out to students that as from the next unit they will not be allowed time to rewrite/copy out rough drafts. They will not after all have time to do this in the exam. The improving section in the next unit will deal specifically with checking and polishing in the exam. If, however, they feel that writing a composition out in 'one go' is going to prove a problem, they may like to start practising with this unit.

Improving your work

Checking and polishing

Students work in pairs to check and polish their work. Allow class time or homework time for this. Remember to use a clear correction code when marking (see page 8).

Planning in the exam

1 Go through the initial explanation with the students. It is important that students set time limits that they feel comfortable with. Some students may prefer to spend more time writing than others, some may prefer longer to improve their work. Allow each student to make their own decisions. They will in any case have time for fine tuning between now and the exam.

2 Let students choose one or two titles and work out rough plans within the planning time limits they have set themselves. Go round checking and helping. Ask them to work in pairs and look at each other's plans offering help and advice where necessary.

Unit 12 **Getaway**

If you have given sufficient coverage to prepositions, you may wish to omit 'Prepositions following adjectives' or deal with it separately later. Alternatively you may feel it gives useful extra practice. If you are short of time the second planning activity can be done for homework as well as the exam question.

Preview

Nominate the groups and give students time to decide on a holiday for each member of the group, including themselves. If the class does not divide into sixes, make smaller groups but decrease the number of holidays accordingly.

Planning 1

For students who have already done the 'spidergraph' exercise in Unit 4 this will be a fairly straightforward exercise. Remind them that they have to add some ideas of their own.

For other students explain how the 'spidergraph' is a useful way of organising information into groups, and of avoiding a jumbled and disorganised set of facts.

It is worth pointing out to all students that this is a particularly useful way of planning a description of a place, where there is not necessarily any 'natural' or 'sequential' order in which to arrange one's ideas.

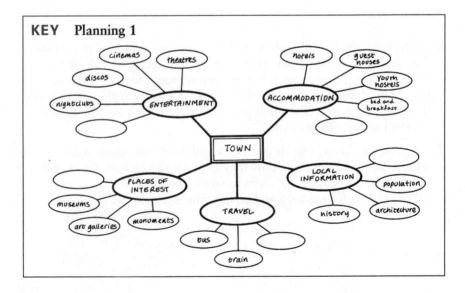

KEY Planning 1

Organising descriptions

1 This is an example of a description of the Potala Palace, Lhasa, Tibet taken from *Danziger's Travels* by Nick Danziger. Stress that students should read for the general idea and not worry about individual vocabulary items. It is a good example of how a description can be organised but you should stress that it is by no means the only way. The point to emphasise is that it is an ordered, organised description. It starts with a view of the Potala from a distance, moves into the entrance, along the passageways, through the rooms and into the heart of the palace – the shrine of the Dalai Lamas.

KEY Organising descriptions

1 1 a) the view of the Potala from a distance
 b) from the distant view to the entrance and just inside
 c) a general description of the inside
 d) a detailed description of the decor inside
 e) the 'heart' of the palace

 2 To create a 'focusing' or 'panning-in' effect or to describe aspects of the palace in the order that the traveller/visitor to the palace sees them.

 3 No. He finishes with it.

 4 *Some possible answers:* unspoilt enormous vast wide thick magnificent superb dominant rich

 5 sight – Point out that other descriptions of places may have a different emphasis though.

 6 (open answer)

---

2 Students should then plan a description of a famous place near where they are now. Stress that they do not have to follow the same organisation as the description here and that they should experiment with different organisations. Allow students a few minutes to do this and to compare their answers with one another. Then have a feedback session to compare different patterns of organisation.

Prepositions following adjectives

1 Students work individually to complete the phrases. Set a time limit of three minutes.

2 Put students in pairs to complete the sentences.

3 Check that students are using the correct preposition.

```
KEY    Prepositions following adjectives
1 by      from      by      with      with
2 1 with      3 of      5 for      7 to      9 for
  2 to        4 to      6 with     8 of
3 with      of      for
```

Suggested answers:

generous similar related	to		familiar pleased angry	with
capable fond aware	of		famous responsible suitable	for

Suggest that students keep prepositions following adjectives in boxes organised like this, or in a similar way, in their notebooks, and that they continue to add to their lists as they come across other combinations.

Planning 2

Students should plan their compositions using a 'spidergraph'. Allow them time to compare their plans and make any improvements.

Exam question (description)

You can set this for homework or allow time in class. Remind students to organise their description carefully and pay attention to prepositions.

Improving your work

Checking and polishing

Students work in pairs to check and polish their work. Allow class time or homework time for this. Remember to use a clear correction code (see page 8).

Checking and polishing in the exam

Go through the notes with the class. Make sure each student decides how long they want to spend on checking in the exam.

Make sure that any compositions done in class are done under exam time conditions and that students get used to allowing themselves time to check through their work making any necessary alterations.

Unit 13 **Crime doesn't pay**

An alternative procedure for this unit is to set 'Making your writing more interesting' as homework before the lesson, and check the answers in class. If you are short of time, the second planning activity can be done as homework as well as the exam question.

Preview

Put students into groups to do this exercise. Check students know the difference between corporal and capital punishment. Encourage students not simply to add *not* to the sentences but to try and make more positive changes that reflect the views of their groups. Some groups may have to agree to differ.

Have a feedback session to compare the views of different groups and continue any relevant discussion.

Planning 1

Discuss the first passage with the class as a whole. Elicit as many ideas as possible as to the setting of the story, the characters and how it might continue. Then put the students into pairs and ask them to do the same with the other two. Let students compare their ideas with other pairs. If there is time, have a feedback session to elicit and compare different ideas. You might also want students to develop one of the storylines further.

For reference: A is from *The Veiled One* by Ruth Rendell; B from *Meet Me At The Morgue* by Ross MacDonald; and C from *The Talented Mr Ripley* by Patricia Highsmith.

Using direct speech in narratives

1 Explain that the first exercise involves students working out the punctuation rules of direct speech on their own. Put students in pairs to do it. Go through the answers checking that everyone has got them right. (The passage is adapted from *The Janus Murder Case* by Colin Wilson.)

2 Then ask students to use the rules they have just worked out to do the second exercise. (This passage is from *Last Seen Wearing* by Colin Dexter.)

KEY Using direct speech in narratives

1 1 b 2 a b c d 3 a 4 b 5 c

2 *The correctly punctuated passage is as follows:*

'You don't like me much, do you, Inspector?'

'I wouldn't say that,' replied Morse defensively. 'It's just that you've never got into the habit of telling me the truth, have you?'

'I've made up for it now, I hope.'

'Have you?' Morse's eyes were hard and piercing, but to his question there was no reply.

'Shall I sign it now?'

Morse remained silent for a while. 'You think it's better this way?' he asked very quietly. But again there was no reply, and Morse passed across the statement and stood up. 'You've got a pen?'

Sheila Phillipson nodded, and opened her long, expensive leather bag.

Making your writing more interesting

1 Ask the students to find words to do with *see* in passage C of 'Planning 1'. They should be able to find: *glanced, saw, noticed, eyeing, looked.* Point out that their writing will be much more interesting if they do not always use the obvious, simple words such as *see, walk* and *say.*

2 Ask students to suggest suitable alternatives to the three words, *walk, say* and *see.* Then get them to find as many as they can in the three word squares below. This can be done as a routine exercise or it can be done as a race – the first students to find all the words (or the most within a given time limit) is the winner. Alternatively, students can be put into threes, each person taking one square and then telling the other two what they have found.

KEY Making your writing more interesting

2 *walk:* run wander stroll dash hurry rush
chase tiptoe

say: advise promise admit accuse insist
shout suggest argue

look: notice glance eye stare peer gaze
watch glimpse

---

3 Now check students understand all the words and ask them to use some of the words they have found to improve the passage. If there is time, get students to compare their answers.

Planning 2

Draw students' attention to the exam question and get them to draft the first few sentences. They should exchange sentences with a partner and then speculate as to how each other's stories might develop. If they wish, they can then incorporate those suggestions into their plan.

Finally they should draw up a flow diagram (see Unit 1) putting in the main events of the story.

Exam question (narrative)

You can set this for homework or allow time in class. Remind students to punctuate any direct speech carefully, and to try and use interesting language where possible.

Improving your work

Checking and polishing

Students work in pairs to check and polish their work. Encourage students to work within the time limits they have set themselves in the previous unit. Remember to use a clear correction code when marking (see page 8).

Writing the correct number of words

Go through the notes with the class. Check students are aware of roughly how much space 150–180 words takes up. Ask them to check back over the last few compositions to see how well they have been doing as regards length.

Unit 14 **Customer relations**

You may wish to deal with the section on the past in sequence separately, or use it for diagnostic purposes. If you are short of time, the second planning section can be done as homework along with the exam question.

Preview

This is a light-hearted introduction to the function of complaining, which this unit deals with. Get students to compare their scores and discuss what is acceptable practice in their country or countries as far as complaining is concerned. What do people complain about? How do they complain? Who do they complain to? etc.

Planning 1

This is the second of the selection exercises. Ask students to read the list of points and choose the ones they would mention. Go through the answers allowing discussion to develop if students disagree.

KEY Planning 1

Probable answer – cross out the following:

- My wife was wearing her new dress.
- Lobster was not on the menu. (Restaurants are not obliged to serve lobster!)
- The napkins did not match the tablecloth.
- Our table was near the door to the street. (Someone has to sit there.)
- The person at the next table was smoking. (Depends if it is a non-smoking table/restaurant.)
- The waiter was not wearing a tie.

Linking words for attitude

Preteach any words that you feel students will be unfamiliar with. Ask students to choose the best word or phrase in the boxes. Get students to compare their answers before going through them with the class.

> **KEY**   Linking words for attitude
>
> 1 to be honest   6 Apparently
> 2 To my surprise   7 clearly
> 3 Fortunately   8 obviously
> 4 unfortunately   9 To make matters worse
> 5 Personally   10 Naturally

The past in sequence

1 Allow students to study the two sentences and elicit from them the reasons for the use of the past perfect.
Sentence 1: generally the past perfect is used when one wants to emphasise that one action followed another; **after** can be used instead of **when**; there may be a period of some time between the actions.
Sentence 2: the simple past is usually used when the second action is an immediate reaction to the first or when the two actions happen at almost the same time.

2 Check students' understanding of the concept and then ask them to complete the exercise.

> **KEY**   The past in sequence
>
> **2** 1 When she saw the fly in her soup, . . .
>   2 When/After the waiter had brought my steak, . . .
>   3 When she saw the advertisement, . . .
>   4 When/After the plane had taken off, . . .
>   5 When/After we had taken our washing to the launderette, . . .
>   6 When our washing finished, . . . (*After our washing had finished,* . . . is possible but with a different emphasis)
>   7 When I saw the dog . . . , . . .
>   8 When I picked up the newspaper, . . .
>   9 When she arrived at the hotel, . . .

Planning 2

Make sure students mix up the sentences they write. Encourage them to think of unsuitable points that are only just unsuitable rather than totally impossible. Have a feedback session to deal with any queries.

Exam question (formal letter)

Set this for homework or allow class time. You should plan on students doing enough timed practice compositions (preferably in class where they cannot cheat on the time!) so that they will be thoroughly familiar with the timing that will be necessary in the exam.

Improving your work

Checking and polishing

Make sure students keep to their personal time limits for checking their answers.

Brief and accurate writing

Allow students to discuss the three passages in pairs and then open the discussion up for a class feedback session. Make sure the class understand that the second answer is the best. Elicit the mistakes in the first answer:

- omission of the day or date
- omission of the type of appliance
- the sequence of events (it sounds as though it was bought in the full knowledge that the knob was missing!)

Elicit the irrelevant items in the last passage:

- the day *or* date (to put both is unnecessary)
- the fact that the person looked at a number of models
- the colour
- finishing other shopping
- the long-winded expression for volume control knob

Draw students' attention to Exam Tip 34.

Unit 15 Food for thought

The second planning activity can be done for homework along with the exam question, if you are short of time.

Preview

This preview section revises some common food vocabulary and gets students to consider the issue of healthy and unhealthy foodstuffs.

Planning 1

This second 'brainstorming' activity (see Unit 3 for the first) can either be done as a timed class exercise or, more entertainingly, as a race to see which student can list the most items in the time allowed.

Giving and justifying opinions

Before students open their books, explain the situation and elicit opinions from students as to which plan they think is best and why. Encourage them to think of arguments for and against the different plans and write them on the board.

1 This is a quick comprehension check. Ask students to read the extracts from the letters and fill in the table.

2 Then get students to look more carefully at the language used in the letters by extracting the relevant phrases and writing them in the boxes.

3 Finally students should write their own opinion supported by arguments. They should then compare their opinions with those of other students. Make sure that students take brief notes of their classmates' opinions as they will need these in the next section.

Key ➡

KEY   Giving and justifying opinions

1

fast food restaurant	A F
health food store	B D E
private club	C

2 *Expressing opinions:* In my opinion . . .   I feel that . . .
In my view . . .   My feeling is that . . .   I think that . . .
It seems to me that . . .

Giving reasons: . . . as . . .   . . . so . . .   . . . because . . .
. . . since . . .   . . . therefore . . .

Reporting opinions

When writing reports students may have to report their own experience.
However, they may also have to report on and summarise the opinions
of other people. This section looks at the language of reporting
opinions. Note that all the reporting verbs in this section follow the
structure *verb* + *that*. Be careful when introducing verbs which demand
a different sentence structure and make sure that students know how
these verbs behave.

1 This is a brief comprehension check. Ask students to read through the
extracts quickly and fill in the table.

2 Students should now read the extracts more carefully and write down
the verbs used to report opinions. When they have done this, go
through the answers and elicit more similar verbs from the class. Add
to the list any further verbs which you think students would find
useful.

3 Students should now refer back to their notes from the previous
section and use a variety of verbs to report their classmates' opinions.

Key ➡

KEY Reporting opinions

1

	FOR	AGAINST
fast food restaurant	D G	A
health food store	F G	C
private club		B
other	E	

2 *(from the texts)* predict   argue   comment   believe   feel
consider   suggest   think

(possible additions) agree   claim   complain   admit   mention   say

Planning 2

This planning exercise gets students to use the 'brainstorming'
techniques they practised in 'Planning 1' to prepare for the exam
question. If you are setting the exam question to be done in class, you
will probably want them to do the planning under exam conditions too.
It may be necessary to remind students of some of the other possible
planning techniques. If so, refer them to the map of the book.

Exam question (report)

This can be done for homework or in class.

Improving your work

Checking and polishing

If the composition has been written in class, the checking stage will be
part of the timed practice. Otherwise make sure that students keep to
their time limits when checking their work.

Managing time in the exam

Students will have already made rough calculations as to how long they
intend to spend on each question. Now that they have answered one or
two questions in exam-type conditions they will have a better idea how
to divide up their time.

Work through the plan with the class making sure that each student
decides on a personal time plan. The times can be flexible, in other
words planning can take 5–10 minutes depending on the question, but
the plan must be clear.

Check that each student has devised a reasonable and intelligent plan.

Unit 16 Literary figures

You may wish to omit the section on relative clauses and deal with it later. Alternatively, you may use it for diagnostic purposes, or for revision.

Preview/Planning 1

Before students open their books, ask them what sort of books they read and how they decide what they are going to read. Elicit opinions from different members of the class. Then ask them to do the Preview activity. When they have finished, they can compare their answers with a partner and/or you can have a class feedback session to find out what most people in the class do.

Getting the reader's attention

1 Leading on from the Preview activity, find out from the class what type of writing makes them sit up and take notice. Make a list on the board of ideas that you elicit. Ask students to read the four short passages and answer the questions.

2 Students should look again at the passages and decide which quotes match which passage.

Students should be encouraged to agree with all the quotes.

KEY   Getting the reader's attention

1 The first and second paragraphs are the most attention getting. The first because it starts with an unusual opinion, the second because the use of rhetorical question arouses one's interest. The fourth is less attention seeking and less conversational but is nonetheless a reasonable beginning to an article. The third is far too long and rambling.

2 a 3   b 1, 2   c 1   d 4   e 1, (2)   f 1   g 1   h 4

Relative clauses

1 Ask students to read through the sentences and underline the relative clauses.

2 Now get students to answer the three questions about the sentences.

3 Students should now be able to complete the table.

4 Read out one or two more sentences containing relative clauses and ask students if they are *identifying* or *non-identifying* in order to check that they understand the concept.
  – Fagin, who is a character in Oliver Twist, was a pickpocket and a thief.
  – The man who wrote this book died last year.
  – The book I enjoyed most was the crime thriller.
  – The book about Neil Armstrong's life, which I gave you for Christmas, has become a bestseller.

KEY   Relative clauses

1 a) The person <u>who wrote that book</u> lived in Antibes.
  b) Phillip Swallow, <u>who is a university lecturer</u>, travels to a conference in the United States.
  c) You would like the romantic novel <u>which I bought for my sister</u>.
  d) The book <u>which would interest you most</u> is *Cry The Beloved Country*.
  e) This novel, <u>which I read last week</u>, has a wonderful plot.

2 a) b e
  b) b e
  c) a c d

3

Type of relative clause defining/non-defining	defining	non-defining
sentence letters	a c d	b e

4 1 I liked that book by Graham Greene which I read last month.
  2 John Grisham, who writes legal dramas, is the world's best-selling author.
  3 Count Fosco, who is a character in Wilkie Collins' *The Woman In White*, is one of literature's most evil creations.
  4 Jack Stanton, who is the 'hero' of *Primary Colors*, closely resembles a real US president.
  5 The book which my sister would like is the biography of Virginia Woolf.

Planning 2

Students can do the planning activity on their own or in pairs. Go round helping with ideas and language if necessary.

Exam question (article)

This can be done in class or for homework. Students may write about the set book if they wish.

Improving your work

Checking and polishing

Students should work out how long they intend to allow themselves for checking and polishing in the exam and then spend that amount of time going over their work.

Reading and answering the question

Allow students a few minutes to read and discuss the texts in pairs. Then have a class discussion. Make sure the following points emerge.

1 – This does not really say which ending the reader preferred.
2 – This does not say why the ending was not as the reader expected.
3 – This text is best; it answers all parts of the question.

Text 3 will get the highest marks; texts 1 and 2 would probably lose marks in proportion to the amount of the question they have ignored. It is a good idea to encourage students to underline the important parts of the question, so that they do not forget to answer any of it.

Unit 17 **Stay healthy!**

You may wish to omit the section on inversion and deal with it separately. If you are short of time, students can do the second planning activity for homework along with the exam question.

Preview

This topic is a quick walk-round activity to arouse interest in the topic of health. Deal with any interesting points that arise in a class feedback session.

Planning 1

1 Get students to start filling in the boxes on their own. If they seem to get stuck, put them into pairs or small groups to exchange ideas. Have a feedback session to go through all the information.

KEY Planning 1	
Possible answers:	
Medical care	*Diet*
– improved facilities – available to more people – people are more aware – increasing emphasis on preventive medicine	– people eat more healthily – more food available (in the West, anyway) – more varied diet possible now
Fitness	*Education*
– more concern over fitness – fitness training is popular as a leisure activity – sporting heroes act as role models	– more people are educated – greater education = more knowledge of health – more educated people realise the value of health

2 Invite opinion as to how the composition might be organised leading students towards an answer like this: introduction, medical care, diet, fitness, education, conclusion. The introduction and conclusion are fixed, and the number and content of the intervening paragraphs will depend on what students feel are the most important areas.

Writing a paragraph

1 When students have done the exercise, point out that paragraphs generally revolve around a topic sentence. This sentence is often the first (but may be in the middle or even at the end). The other sentences will illustrate and develop the topic sentence in a clear and logical way. The paragraph in this question should be seen as an illustration of this, not in any way as a model slavishly to be followed.

KEY   Writing a paragraph

1 Sentence 1 – topic sentence
    Sentence 2 – illustrations 1 and 2
    Sentence 3 – example of illustration 2
    Sentence 4 – illustration 3
    Sentence 5 – result of illustration 3

---

2 Ask students to produce a paragraph of their own from the notes in 'Planning 1' and then exchange and analyse each other's paragraphs. Go round checking and helping students while they do this. Have a feedback session at the end if necessary.

Inversion

1 Give students a few minutes to study the sentences. Elicit the fact that the 'not only' has been moved to the beginning of the sentence and this has caused the inversion of the subject and the verb. Elicit also that this generally happens in writing rather than speech and it is rather formal, emphasising the words that are brought to the beginning of the sentence. Alert students to the fact that an auxiliary 'do' or 'did' may be needed to form an inversion.

2 Students should underline the examples of subject/verb inversion shown in the speech balloons and circle phrases which cause that inversion.

If you have time, ask students to rewrite the sentences in less formal English, i.e. changing the word order and inverting the subject and verb.

Key ➡

KEY Inversion

2

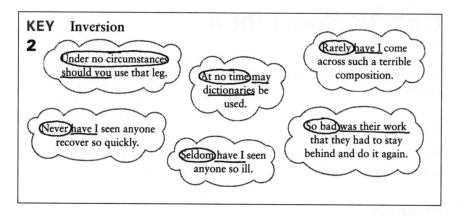

Under no circumstances should you use that leg.

At no time may dictionaries be used.

Rarely have I come across such a terrible composition.

Never have I seen anyone recover so quickly.

Seldom have I seen anyone so ill.

So bad was their work that they had to stay behind and do it again.

3 Students should write a paragraph about an imaginary, unhealthy person. Encourage them to use the phrases they circled above, and to be as imaginative as possible.

Planning 2

Get students to use boxes similar to those in 'Planning 1' to plan their answers. Get them to compare notes and plan their compositions.

Exam question (discussion essay)

Set this for homework or allow time in class.

Improving your work

Checking and polishing

Allow students only their own time limit for checking and polishing their work.

Checking in the exam

Get students to look back over their most recent compositions and note down their most frequent mistakes. Make sure they look especially for these when checking their compositions. Make sure that they know to look out for mistakes like these in the exam.

Unit 18 Sport for all!

You may wish to omit the section on the gerund and infinitive and deal with it separately. Alternatively you may feel it provides useful further practice.

Preview

Put students into pairs or small groups for discussion. Have a feedback session if time permits.

Planning 1

Remind students that putting things in order of priority is a useful planning technique. Get students to do this exercise on their own and then compare and discuss their answers with a partner.

Combining information

Students may be required to synthesise information from two or more different sources. While other units have indirectly asked students to do this, this unit specifically deals with this skill and gives students practice in it.

Students should work through this exercise on their own and then check their answers with a partner.

	Monday	Tuesday	Wednesday	Thursday	Friday
morning	yoga 10am squash	judo 11am squash	T'ai Chi 10–12.30 squash	aerobics 11am squash	T'ai Chi 10–12.30 squash
afternoon	weight training 2–5pm jogging from 3pm squash	weight training 2–5pm jogging from 3pm squash	weight training 2–5pm jogging from 3pm cycling 3–5pm squash	weight training 2–5pm jogging from 3pm squash	weight training 2–5pm jogging from 3pm squash
evening	judo 7pm squash	football training yoga 6pm squash	badminton from 6pm roller hockey 6–8pm squash	aerobics 8pm squash	cycling 6–8pm roller hockey 6–8pm football match squash

Verbs which take the gerund and/or infinitive

Allow students time to work through the first exercise and complete the boxes in the second exercise. Then go through the answers.

KEY Verbs which take the gerund and/or infinitive

1 1 He began <u>to run</u> . . . ✓
   She began <u>running</u> . . . ✓

   2 . . . she enjoys <u>swimming</u> . . . ✓
   She enjoys <u>to swim</u> . . . ✗

   3 They tried <u>to walk</u> faster . . . ✓
   . . . they tried <u>walking</u> faster . . . ✓

   4 . . . I stopped <u>to look</u> . . . ✓
   I stopped <u>looking</u> . . . ✓

   5 Jim promised <u>to play</u> . . . ✓
   . . . he promised <u>playing</u> . . . ✗

   6 She continued <u>cycling</u> . . . ✓
   She continued <u>to cycle</u> . . . ✓

2

verbs which only take **–ing**	verbs which only take **to + infinitive**
enjoy	promise
verbs which take **–ing** or **to + infinitive** with no change in meaning	verbs which take **–ing** or **to + infinitive** with a change in meaning
begin continue intend	try stop remember

Check that students understand how the verbs in the lower right-hand box change their meaning, depending on whether they take the gerund or the infinitive.

If you **try to do** something, you make an effort to do it. **Try to do** indicates **difficulty** of some sort.

If you **try doing something,** you do it to see if it works or to see if you like it. **Try doing** indicates it is an **experiment** of some sort.

If you **stop to do** something, it means you take a break from something so that you can do something else.

If you **stop doing** something, it means that you are doing it, and you stop.

If you **remember to do** something, you remember what you have to do.

If you **remember doing** something, you remember something that happened in the past.

3 Allow students a few minutes to write sentences, then put them in pairs to compare answers. When they have finished, get them to add the verbs they have used to the boxes. Encourage them to add other examples as they come across them over the next few weeks.

Planning 2

The purpose of this exercise is to refresh the students' memory of all the different planning techniques that should now be at their disposal.

Ask students to list as many different planning techniques as they can. Put them in pairs to help each other if necessary, and then encourage them to work through the questions and discuss their answers with a partner. Have a class discussion on the usefulness and applicability of the different planning techniques.

Ask students to read the exam question and decide how to plan their answer.

Exam question (formal letter)

Students can do this for homework or in class.

Improving your work

Checking and polishing

Get students to check their work within their own time limits. Draw their attention to Exam Tip 44.

The future

Allow students to read through the suggestions and discuss ideas with a partner. Have a feedback session to find out what everyone has decided.

Review unit

How much do you know about the exam?

A quick check that everyone knows what is expected of them is usually worthwhile. In our experience there is usually someone who has forgotten what is required.

KEY How much do you know about the exam?

1 false – two
2 true
3 false – no dictionaries
4 false – not in the new exam
5 false – you <u>may</u> have to write a letter
6 false – the question in Part 1 is compulsory. There is no choice.
7 false – you can answer a question about the set book if you want
8 true
9 false – they do not count each mistake
10 true

How much do you remember about planning?

KEY How much do you remember about planning?

flow diagram/order of events	→ narratives
order of priority	→ discussion essays/reports
listing questions	→ letters/reports/articles
'spidergraph'	→ descriptions/discussion essays/reports/articles
listing advantages and disadvantages	→ discussion essays
questionnaires	→ discussion essays/reports
'brainstorming'	→ all types
selecting points	→ all types
'headlights'	→ discussion essays
opening sentences	→ narratives/articles
boxes	→ discussion essays

Above is a list of the most likely combinations. Point out that it is not definitive; other combinations may work well too.

How much do you remember about the Exam Tips?

Check that students are able to recall the advice they have been given.
Page references for appropriate tips are as follows.

KEY   How much do you remember about the Exam Tips?

punctuation (page 18)   layout (pages 41, 54, 100)
interest (pages 79, 80)   handwriting (page 51)
structure (pages 11, 69)   time (pages 71, 93)
personalisation (page 32)   beginnings and endings (pages 60, 96)
relevance (pages 47, 63)   brief and accurate writing (page 87)

How prepared are you?

1 Allow students to work through the questions. Then have a feedback
session comparing answers and suggesting improvements.

2 Then ask students to consider the next two questions.

Students can make their plans in class or do that as a final homework
exercise. Get them to compare their answers and suggest
improvements.

KEY   How prepared are you?

1 1 a) letter of complaint
     b) listing questions

   2 a) narrative
     b) flow diagram/ordering events

   3 a) discussion essay
     b) listing advantages & disadvantages/'headlights'

   4 a) report
     b) listing questions/questionnaire

2 *Possible answers for a):*
   1 layout, past tenses, connectives of attitude
   2 past tenses, time linking words
   3 language of advantages and disadvantages
   4 layout, language/style of reports

How good are you at polishing your work?

Allow students time on their own (and then in pairs if you wish).
A possible answer is below.

---

197 Woodstock Road
Oxford OX2 7AB
12th February 1999

Dear Sir or Madam,

I am writing to you because I saw your advert in an Orientation Center and I would like some more information.

At the moment I am a student in France but I will finish my studies this year. Following this, I would like to go to the United States to improve my English, since I want to work in tourism. In addition, I would like to learn about American History. Please could you let me know if it is possible to study this subject on request and what level of English is required?

I would also be grateful if you would tell me how many hours per week your courses are and, if I want to stay for three months, when I might start. You do not give exact prices so perhaps you could send me precise details of fees for the courses that I am interested in.

Finally I would appreciate it if you would send me further information about the type of accommodation available and whether it is included in the price.

I am looking forward to your response.

Yours faithfully
Carole Pointereau

Good points about the original letter are:
- its layout
- its organisation: each paragraph has a clear topic
- it answers the question fully and also gives additional information
- it is extremely legible
- it does not have too many grammatical mistakes
- the length is good (160 words)

Areas for the student to improve/concentrate on:
- articles
- formal language of requests
- use of linkers, e.g. However, Finally, etc.

[You may photocopy this page to give to your students.]